Oct 24-26th 2003 (the King & I week-end)

To Allison

lots of good memories

love Mom x

THIS LAND I LOVE

WATERLOO COUNTY

THIS LAND I LOVE

Waterloo County

CARL HIEBERT

CATALOGUING IN PUBLICATION DATA

Hiebert, Carl E., 1947–
This land I love: Waterloo County

ISBN 1-55046-362-4

1. Waterloo (Ont.: County) — Aerial photographs.
2. Waterloo (Ont.: County) —
Description and travel. 3. Mennonites — Ontario —
Waterloo (County) — Social life and customs. I. Title.

FC3095.W38H53 2000   779'.997134404   C00-931212-9
F1059.W32H53 2000

Published by
GIFT OF WINGS PUBLISHING
556 Fallingbrook Drive
Waterloo, Ontario
N2L 4N4
519-884-1194

www.carlhiebert.com
giftofwings@look.ca

*Part of the proceeds from the
sale of this book will be donated to charity.*

Design by Gillian Stead
Printed in Canada

Acknowledgments

This Land I Love has unfolded gradually over a twelve-year period. Although much of the work was completed alone, I am grateful to those who helped this book to become a reality:

Parry and the Weber family, for generously giving me and my ultralight our "summer home." Most of these pictures were taken within just five miles of the 600-foot runway out behind the barn. A finer, grassroots airport could not be found anywhere.

My friends, for their insightful editorial feedback, especially Kim Morouney and Gerry Forwell.

Nancy Martin, my true ear to the Mennonite community. Her kindness, understanding and words of wisdom have proven invaluable. I am also honoured that she agreed to write the foreword for this book.

Gill Stead and Noel Hudson, design and edit team second to none. This represents my third book designed by Gill. Her work only gets better.

The rural Mennonites of Waterloo County. Sitting in your shops and kitchens listening to your stories is one of the best ways anyone could spend a Saturday. Most important of all, your earthbound art is a gift to me. I hope we'll continue to wave at each other for a long time to come.

Thank you all.

*The stories that accompany the photographs in this book
were told to me by Waterloo County Mennonites.*

To the Mennonite community of Waterloo County —
the farmers and gardeners, the tillers and artisans.
Your nurturing of this land has given me the land I love.

Foreword

The countryside of Waterloo County is dotted with many Mennonite family farms. Most of them are comfortable and prosperous-looking, with the buildings in a setting of mature trees, fruitful fields, orchards and gardens.

Mennonite people feel close to their land. They consider it a sacred trust to nurture and improve their farms, to make them productive and to provide food for the hungry world. As an Old Order Mennonite, born and raised in Waterloo County, I feel privileged to be a part of this heritage. Driving down a county road in an open buggy, you get the full benefit of the sights, sounds and smells of our countryside.

My father was a child when his parents moved here in 1918. He remembers helping herd the cattle over eight miles to this larger farm. There was very little motor traffic then. Now his four-year-old great-grandson looks out at the cows in the pasture and knows each one by name. So the cycle continues.

In spring, there is always a sense of urgency to work outdoors, either in the fields or gardens. It is so rewarding to see the first greening on the land and realize that another growing season is underway.

Many of the seeds planted in the garden date back to my grandmother's time. Remembering that she planted the parent seeds in this same garden gives me a feeling of continuity in the cycle of life. I think ahead to future gardens as I watch my nephew's children help pull the weeds or enjoy a fresh carrot.

Spring is also when we expect Carl Hiebert to be back with his ultralight. Carl has become a well-known figure among many people in our community, and to some of us, a valued friend. In early spring we listen for

the sound of his plane. When he zooms past and waves at us, we know he is busy photographing the countryside and soaking in the atmosphere. He approaches each flight with such anticipation and exuberance. Carl has an uncanny ability to visualize what will make an arresting picture. The changing patterns and vivid colours are a continual feast for the eye.

In this book, both the writing and the photographs are a joy. His introduction notes show an appreciative sensitivity and understanding of our Mennonite way of life. Carl's love of this land comes through very clearly in this book, as well as his integrity as a person. *This Land I Love* is a treasure.

Nancy Martin

Introduction

It's mid-July when I return home from a trip to Africa. I take a day to recover from the inevitable jetlag then head out to Weber's farm in bad need of my Waterloo County aerial fix. Several years ago I taught Ed and Parry Weber, father and son, how to fly. In return, they generously allowed me to build a hangar and fly my ultralight from their farm, just a mile west of Elmira, in the heart of traditional Mennonite country.

It's late afternoon when I pull my dusty machine out of the hangar. Winds are light, the sky cloudless — a perfect day for aerial sightseeing. I smile as my motorcycle of the skies effortlessly sheds gravity's grip and rises above the 600-foot grass runway. It is as though I am discovering flight for the first time. What an outrageous freedom this is. One of my heroes, Leonardo Da Vinci — sculptor, architect, artist, designer, engineer — had a passionate lifelong preoccupation with flight. I hear his words now as I carve through the sky: "Once having tasted flight, you will walk this earth with your eyes turned skyward, for there you have been and there you long to return."

As I have done countless times before, I instinctively bank southwest toward the quiet village of Hawkesville. The sight of the meandering Conestogo River, the rolling fields and the concentration of Mennonite farms brings me joy, especially today. I love this land because it brings me home to myself. Flying over these farms makes me feel that, if I belong anywhere, it is here.

It's been almost five weeks since I've flown this path, and during that time, the land has undergone a magical transformation. The fields below touch me with their colours, textures and designs, and with the beauty of their purpose. Twice now, I have flown across Canada in my open-cockpit ultralight, taking thousands of pictures en route, yet nothing, absolutely nothing, can surpass the lushness of Waterloo County.

I am intoxicated by this finest of earthbound tapestries. Tears come. Tears of gratitude, of privilege and of feeling blessed in this unsullied view of creation. I realize I love this land like nowhere else on the planet.

The book you hold in your hands is my attempt to share my love of this place with others

In ten years of flying over Waterloo County, I've developed a renewed awareness of how life rotates through the seasons. As urban dwellers, it is easy to lose some of our sensitivity to seasonal changes. We move from air-conditioned homes and cars in summer to digitally set thermostats in winter. But there is no blurring of the seasons for those who till the soil — or for that matter, for us fair-weather pilots in open-cockpit flying machines. I feel a certain kinship with my friends who cultivate the earth. For us, the melting spring snows signal a new season of opportunities. Even after more than 2,500 hours of piloting ultralights, thoughts of the year's first flights obsess me in spring. Invariably, I'm reminded of being back in grade school and wrestling with the temptation to play hooky. Each year I can hardly contain my enthusiasm as I fill the five-gallon gas tank and preflight the aircraft.

Such flights serve as a warm-up routine for the longer, more satisfying flights of summer. But what joy to spend half an hour wheeling and dancing in the skies without the heavy woolen shirt, down vest, leather flight jacket and the worry about frostbite. I often hang two cameras from my neck but expect little in the way of compelling images. Even on the brightest of early spring days, the land is in transition and feels sluggish somehow. The last remnants of snow hide behind fence rows, ditches, and on the north sides of buildings. Many of the fields bare their black furrows, and last year's pastures sweep by in expanses of brown. Ice melts in the faster flowing sections of the river, and spring runoff begins.

At least two characteristics define Waterloo County farmland. First, conservative Mennonite farms are typically 100 acres in size — small by regional standards — and support a variety of crops. If I fly ten miles away from the heart of this community in any direction, I know I will encounter huge single-crop fields, 50- or perhaps 100-acre expanses of corn or soybeans. The green often seems to stretch to the horizon and leaves little to excite me. But here, a single farm may grow six different plots, including wheat, oats, corn and pasture. Each field produces its own palette of colour and texture, particularly as the crops approach maturity.

The second distinction is the use of farming techniques that largely disappeared sixty years ago. Two conservative farming groups dominate the area, the Old Order Mennonites and the Dave Martin Mennonites. Some refer to both denominations as the "horse-and-buggy" Mennonites and incorrectly group them together. (see page 121 for clarification). Dave Martin Mennonites and a few of the ultra-conservative Old Order Mennonites still use workhorses to till their soil. Nothing charms me more than seeing a team of five burly Clydesdales cutting fresh black furrows through a green pasture.

Horses are relatively lightweight compared to tractors, so as the fields slowly begin to dry under the spring sun, the hitched teams of Clydesdales and Percherons are among the first signals of another cycle of the seasons. As early as mid-April, the fieldwork begins. The cultivator makes the first brushstroke across the grey landscape. Its steel fingers ripple the surface crust and invite warm spring breezes to breathe life into the newly exposed soil. For several weeks, the farmer and Old Man Weather play their perennial game of tug-of-war. With a wary eye on the clouds building in the east, the farmer loads his seed drill and hopes to finish his ten-acre field before another spring rain catches him — just two more rounds to go. It may only take three days to seed the spring crops, but inclement weather can easily extend the job to four or five weeks.

Rains also hurry the earliest harvest of the year, the first cut of hay. Lush green strands of sweet-smelling alfalfa, clover and timothy fall almost soundlessly behind freshly sharpened mower blades. On sunny days,

farmers seem jubilant as they circle rhythmically around their fields. They wave as I glide overhead. How does one begin to describe the charged smell of drying hay? Even at 2,000 feet, a mid-afternoon thermal can waft that sweet, memory-laden aroma upward and carry me back to my childhood and haying seasons on my family's own Mennonite farm.

The climax of summer is not a date circled on any calendar or found in *The Farmer's Almanac*, it comes with the grain harvest. For the aerial photographer, nothing surpasses the simple beauty of just-stooked sheaves of wheat and oats. The harvest begins when horse-drawn grain binders transform fields of swaying gold into thousands of scattered sheaves tied in single wraps of binder twine. The scene differs little from a hundred years ago. Men with pitchforks still create agricultural art from freshly cut fields. Five or seven individual sheaves are systematically stacked together in groups called stooks, their grain-laden heads pointed skyward to the drying sun.

I float over fields bathed in the bronzed light of late evening, and the patterns below make me think of a parade, with row upon row of marchers standing at attention, awaiting the next commands. They will hold their ranks patiently for days, until the horse-drawn wagons arrive and skillfully wielded pitchforks send them arching up onto the load, off to the barn and then to the threshing machines.

In just one day, an entire field can be swept clean of its design. The wagons keep arriving, the rows disappear, and too soon, the field is empty. It is only late July, but the clipped stubble suggests that summer is racing by too quickly. A friend tells me of a generations-old Pennsylvania-Dutch expression: *Wann de wind iwwe die haawe schtubble blosst, noht is de summer am geh.* "When the wind blows through the oat stubble, the summer is on its way out."

Photographing these patterns with a combination of soft light and gentle winds is an annual test of my patience. The windows of opportunity can be challengingly brief. One year, my best images of the entire harvest occurred in just one evening. Harvest had been underway for a week, but the skies had been heavy with humidity and haze. The flat light makes strong, sparkling images impossible. Then, serendipity. Late on a Saturday afternoon, a small cold front rolled through, leaving behind it crystal-clear light. Exactly what I'd been waiting for. I immediately cancelled a dinner invitation and headed for the farm with high expectations. I was not disappointed. In just under an hour, I took eight rolls of film — over 250 pictures. Several of them appear in this book, including the photograph on page 41.

As compelling as this landscape may be, its people mean even more to me. Over the years, I have built relationships with a number of Mennonite families. Now, as I fly overhead, hands wave everywhere — men with their horses, women in their gardens, children at play. Sometimes, on a summer evening's flight, I feel I'm in a receiving line at a joyous ceremony. Scarcely do I pass over one farm before I see figures waving in the next.

I feel a particular connection with the children of this county, many of whom appeared in one of my previous photography books, *Us Little People*. They now dash around their houses, trying to keep me in sight between the treetops as I flash by overhead. I often recognize their individual faces and am reminded of how fortunate I am to see their world from both the ground and the air.

But the barefoot season ends, and the children don socks and shoes and head back to school after Labour Day weekend. There is a sadness for me in this transition to autumn, for it means the best of this aerial smorgasbord is over. Cultivators and ploughs systematically harass once-golden grain fields. Bands of black, freshly turned soil widen across the fields as farmers follow their ploughs from one fence row to the next. At each end, they pause for a couple of minutes, allowing the horses to slow their heavy breathing and cool off just a bit.

Green pastures soon lie dull and dusty. Cornfields that spent their summer waving energetic green leaves at the sky have made a surprisingly quick transition to brown, cobs hardened and yellow, waiting for harvesters. Even the gardens have given up their summer vibrancy. A late September frost saps whatever colours the flowers might have retained. Spades slice into the rows of potatoes, forcing them to yield their sustenance for the long winter ahead. Strawberries are weeded for the last time and tucked in with a blanket of straw to protect them from the icy blasts to come. I sometimes chuckle seeing this from overhead. Shouldn't the meticulous gardeners place pillows under one end of the straw rows, and allow the berries to spend their winter months sleeping just a little more comfortably?

Although the once dense forests of Waterloo County have been largely cleared for agriculture, the early pioneers were prudent enough to leave behind five-to-ten-acre "bush lots" at the backs of their farms. Beyond the ecological soundness of this foresight, maintaining a healthy balance of fields and forests, these lots also provide winter firewood and maple sap in the spring. In many cases, the lots from neighbouring farms are contiguous, resulting in a swath of trees that runs midway between the rural concessions.

As the last sigh of summer ends, groves of maple, beech, poplar, oak and hickory obey their inner clocks and gradually change their dress code. Shortened days cause the production of chlorophyll to cease, and green leaves soon exhibit their autumn colours. Reds, yellows, bronzes, oranges herald autumn's final extravagance. From my aerial vantage point, I sometimes feel I might drown in this profusion of colour. (Ironically, for all its

colourful excess, autumn is the most difficult season to photograph well. Just when a concentration of colour has my attention, I am distracted by yet another burst elsewhere. It's easy to run through three or four rolls of film and not be satisfied with one picture. Perhaps autumns, like sunsets, are too charged with beauty to ever be captured justly on film.)

Walnut, oak and ash are last trees to leaf-out in spring and the last to drop their leaves in the fall. Even after three days of driving rain and wind, these isolated pockets of red and orange still stand guard throughout the bush lots. Some years, their leaves still cling tenaciously even after the first snowfall. When these leaves finally disappear, winter, without question, waits just behind the next grey bank of roiling clouds.

For all its intensity, winter is the season whose arrival is least predictable. Snow may appear in early October or as late as mid-December. The farmer, however, does not have the luxury of gambling on such impetuous scheduling. Crops must be stored, fields ploughed, and winter wheat seeded before the season's first significant freeze. It's a close race some years, but always, and finally, the snows come. And thus begins a quiet in the land. A few horses may charge across a blank white pasture or a manure spreader may chug slowly through the drifts, but mostly, there is a sense that life has disappeared from this place. Groundhogs burrow deep, cows nestle in straw-lined stalls, and the men of the fields retreat to their shops and barns.

I see my friends travelling in their buggies on their way to pick up supplies at the nearest general store or to visit a neighbour, and I realize they have to dress as warmly as I do in my airborne sleigh. Even by picking my flying days carefully, I can only feel reasonably warm if I dress in layers of clothing. Anything more than a half-hour flight and I am inviting frostbite. My fingers suffer the most, because to operate my cameras I can only wear thin, flexible gloves. Changing film is a real challenge. The gloves must come off completely, and I must hang onto my flapping gloves and change film while flying the aircraft with stiff fingers. My eyes tear from the cold and the salty tears freeze on my glasses, reducing visibility.

A day later, however, as I pore over my slides on the light table, I am rewarded for my temporary discomfort. The winter perspective of the land is completely distinctive. Virtually all colours disappear and the world is reduced to simple black and white. Fence lines provide the only distinction between otherwise identical fields. On a sunny day, the trees of an apple orchard become spider tracks or an x-ray (see page 115).

At the most, there are only a handful of days when I might choose to fly during these cold winter months. Yet, surprisingly, I rarely think of it, as if my passion for flying and aerial photography has entered into a form of hibernation. Perhaps the wait is a prerequisite for the focused awareness that accompanies spring and the first flights of the year. Would I be so keen to lose myself in the beauty of this land if I could see it every day? I suspect not.

And so, like the farmer, I wait, absorbed in other worlds of activity as winter drags itself along. Like the farmer, I await the melting snows of spring, when I know we'll meet again. He'll wave as I once more carve through the blue sky above him. We have a tradition to keep. And so we shall, for this land we both love will always be there.

Farming Teaches You

I think there are a lot of advantages to living on the farm. First of all, a husband and wife can be together in raising the children. If Dad disappears to work every day with a lunch bucket, he'll hardly have time to be with his children, and his wife will be left with all the responsibility of the children. The farm is also a good way to keep us close to nature. For example, you don't need to have sex education from a textbook when you have farm animals. All of my children would have seen calves born before they ever went to school.

Farming teaches you that things don't always go as planned and that you have to take life in stride. You could have all your hay cut and you're just getting ready to head out with your tractor to start baling, and the rain comes. Well, you don't cuss and swear. That's just how things are. You soon come to realize that God always takes care of you. That wet hay is going to dry off eventually. Most years we end up with an average crop.

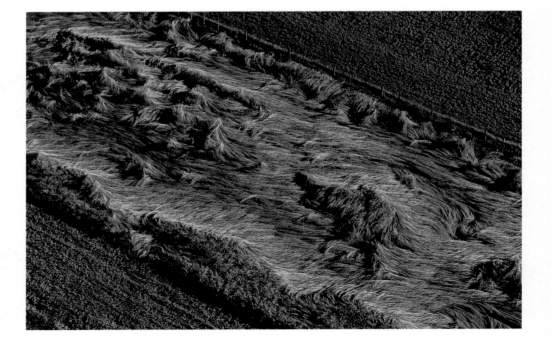

The farm is probably the best place to learn responsibility and how to work at an early age. By the time the boys are ten, they are already taking care of the calves, and the girls are gathering eggs. They might grumble sometimes, but they know that it's important for all of us to work together.

The Best Things

I think my best memories are of spring, when all my older brothers would come home for the sap season. They were hired out on other farms, but at Christmas and in spring we would all be together. I can still remember the fun we had having supper back at the sap shanty. We would get the chores done early and then about seven o'clock, when it was already pitch dark, the children and mom would head back to the bush where the men were working. We would boil eggs in the sap bucket by hanging it in the back pan of the evaporator. Next we'd have wieners. We'd stick them on wires and roast them in front of the stove. There was so much heat the doors would be red-hot. While the men were boiling the sap, we'd play games or sing hymns — mostly in four-part harmony. It was usually after nine before we were ready to head for home. We'd all pack on the sleigh, along with a load of fresh maple syrup and off we'd go across the fields, through the night. What fun that was. I really believe the best things in life are free.

The Dawn Chorus

Among the things that I particularly enjoy are the sounds of spring. Songbirds seem to go wild with joy. We sleep with our windows open, of course, and at 5:30 the birds are in full concert. We call it the "dawn chorus." As the summer advances, the birds sing less and less. Sometimes, in the morning, in the midst of all this cheerful chirping, I hear a *graawk, graawk* as our lone blue heron wings off on his daily flight to the pond. It sounds like he has a sore throat. But he makes up for it when he stands so gracefully at the edge of the pond.

Stone Picking

As I'm planting in spring, I'm already imagining what the crops will look like in the fall. It always strikes me as a miracle, because you never know what's going to happen from one year to the next. It teaches you to live one day at a time.

Once the crops are planted, our next job is stone picking. Every able-bodied person is expected to help. It can actually be fun, even though it's hard work. We all get a chance to talk together. Sometimes the young people of the neighbourhood come together to help pick stones at a farm where help is scarce. This is always quite enjoyable. The stones need to be picked off the work field so valuable machinery is not wrecked during harvest time. Somehow the stones from the Canadian Shield are brought to the surface every spring by frost.

It's amazing how quickly the young children mimic their parents. I remember watching Cleon when he was only two years old. He had taken his little wagon out to the garden and was loading it up with small stones, much the same way he had seen his mother and father picking stones out of the field earlier that spring.

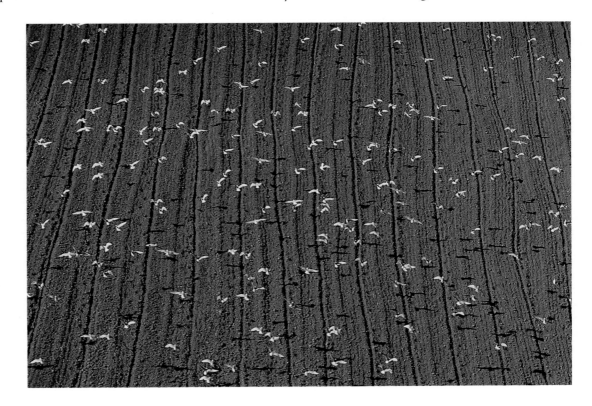

My Favourite Bird

I think my favorite bird is a swallow. I'm always happy to see them return in early May. There is nothing quite like them — and, my, how they swoop down to tease the cats. And the cats certainly have misguided feelings that one of these times they are going to catch one. They never do. What pranksters those birds are. It's always sad when the swallows leave. They begin congregating in late August and will leave in the next few weeks. They love to sit on the hydro lines and wash lines and chatter to each other. One gets the impression they are planning their migratory route. Their chattering reminds me of the poem "Dame Swallow," which goes something like this:

Dame Swallow is a chatterbox

She chatters all day long.

Wherever neighbours meet in flocks

She loves to join the throng.

33

Continuity

I love planting my spring garden. The birds are busy and happy, and I am thankful to be a part of it all. As I plant the pole beans, I think of my grandmother, who planted this kind as well. We've been gathering the same seeds for years now. Just at the edge of the garden is a huge old apple tree which was already here when my father moved here at the age of eleven in 1918. Thinking of this gives me a deep sense of continuity and balance in this spring ritual.

35

The Doddy Haus

Translated directly, *doddy haus* means "grandfather's house." What it really means is a small addition not as large as the original farmhouse. We added two doddy hauses onto our place and now have four generations living here. Usually it's the youngest son who gets the farm, and when he gets married, he moves into the main part of the house. That's when the parents move into an addition built onto the main part of the house. By doing it this way, most old people end up staying on the farm until the end of their years. If the third generation now takes over the farm, the grandparents will move again, this time into the third doddy haus. This is often a mobile home that is connected with a passageway to the main house. You get used to living in a trailer like this. People are sometimes amazed how much entertaining we can do in the small quarters. It must be okay, because they keep coming back.

Garden Talk

Gardens are an important part of our way of living. One sort of plans the garden weeks ahead of time in terms of what crops you're going to plant and the quantity, and where the you'll plant them, since we try to rotate our crops from year to year. Some crops, such as cucumbers or tomatoes, take a lot of nutrients out of the soil, so you have to balance your planting. Sometimes we plant oil radishes for six weeks or so at the end of the growing season, to build up the soil, and then plough them down.

I'm always amazed at how quickly you get returns for your efforts. For example, lettuce can be planted in April, and sometimes you're eating it by late May — which is only five or six weeks. When I go out to pick fruit or vegetables I am often filled with a sense of awe that things grow the way they do. It reminds me of the promise in the Bible. Genesis 8:22 says, "While the earth remains, seedtime and harvest . . . shall not cease."

On a typical summer day, it's easy to spend two or three hours a day in the garden. You do whatever picking you need first thing in the morning when it's still cool, and then you work under the cool shade trees to shell the peas, clean the beans or husk the corn. Sometimes we'll spend just about a whole day out there. It's one of the best things about summer.

I sometimes watch my niece, who is only age five, already helping in the garden. She'll help pick weeds — though that may not last too long. It's more rewarding to pick ground cherries and tomatoes and strawberries.

On Sunday afternoons in the summer, when the women visit — there might be six or seven of us — it's a guarantee we'll talk about our gardens. We will likely talk about two things: what problems we're having, and if anyone has found a solution. For example, one lady had a late ripening of her tomatoes. Someone suggested she remove the late blossoms and suckers in order to speed up the ripening. And it worked. Secondly, we love to share in the joy and talk about the blessings we have. It's wonderful how plentiful everything is. Often we wish we could send the extra that we have directly to people who need it in other parts of the world.

Farm Life

I think the best thing about farm life is that it's a family effort where everyone has a common focus. It's also the best place to learn the importance of how to work. As a boy growing up, I remember one of my first important jobs was taking care of my rabbits. I was responsible for buying the feed, caring for them, and then taking them to the market when they were ready. It was my first chance to earn real money, which I saved up and bought my first bicycle. After the rabbits, I learned how to raise calves, and so learning to care for animals became a natural thing for me. Then, from age sixteen to twenty I worked out on other farms. This is a common practice with us Mennonites.

I think living on the small family farm is going to get more and more difficult in the future. We'll either have to grow specialty crops to increase our income or set up shops. The debt load starting out today is getting way too high and is a big financial challenge.

Good Years and Bad Years

I've farmed for thirty-four years and have seen both good and bad years. But the worst year anyone has ever talked about was in 1816. The story's been passed on from one generation to the next. It was said there was a frost every month that year. The people just kept planting and replanting. Apparently this happened because there was a volcano somewhere in the tropics. It darkened the skies and wouldn't let the sun through, so there was a complete crop failure. All the people had to eat was fish and mush — mush being

a ground-up grain. When they got tired of eating fish and mush, they ate mush and fish. At least they had some variety.

But there were good years, too. I remember one year in the mid-forties when we had a particularly good crop of grain. It must have been three or four feet high. I was on the grain binder, and my brother asked me, "How many sheaves a minute are we getting?" I counted them, and there were fifty-five a minute — almost one a second. That old binder took quite a beating.

West Montrose Covered Bridge

The covered bridge is handy because it's a shortcut to the highway. You might think that since the bridge is covered, the horses would be a bit skittish in going through, but they quickly get used to it. It probably seems like a tunnel to them. The biggest problem we have sometimes are the louvers on the walls of the bridge. If the sun is just right, you get patches of bright light on what is otherwise a dark floor. That's confusing to a horse. It doesn't know if it's a hole in the floor or what.

The bridge comes in especially handy on a Sunday, when we have a service here at our Winterbourne church. When church is out at noon, you might have twenty-five buggies streaming through in a short time. It's wonderful to hear the "clip-clopping" of all those hooves on the wooden planks.

You sometimes wonder about all the tourists. I've seen up to three busloads at once. People will stand right in the middle of the road staring at us through their cameras. If you weren't careful, you'd run them over. What do they really see about us? Just the horse and buggy and our different way of dressing? It almost makes me think I must be in a zoo sometimes.

Turning Over
the Sod

I bought my first farm in 1945 for $6,000 and today it's worth at least half a million. Some of my best memories are of ploughing with the team. With four horses and a two-furrow plough, you could do four to five acres a day. But you don't work them every day. They need a day of rest about every three days or so. There's something very satisfying about turning over the sod and seeing the black dirt that is the beginning of next year's crop.

A Measure of Privacy

All of my daughters now live on farms and I'm grateful for that. On a farm, space provides a measure of privacy. The public may drop in from time to time, and that's all right. In the city, you are surrounded by the public, and maybe privacy can only be obtained by choosing to ignore your neighbours.

Maple Syrup Season

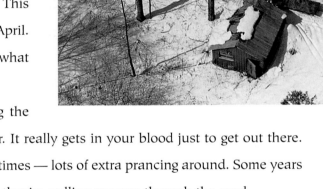

The calendar says January 1 is the beginning of the new year, but for most farmers, maple syrup time signals a new season. When you can see rivulets of water around the barn and when the snow starts to get packy, you start to wonder, "Is it time to tap?" My grandfather used to say, "If you want to know if the sap is running, you have to go and look." This season usually begins in early March and can run into April. What's best are warm days and then freezing at night. That's what makes the sap really run.

Nobody wants to be the "silly goat" and start tapping the trees too early, but you don't want to miss the season either. It really gets in your blood just to get out there. You can even see some initial excitement in the horses sometimes — lots of extra prancing around. Some years they're pulling sleighs in three feet of snow, and other times they're pulling wagons through the mud.

It's a good family activity. As soon as the children get home from school and change, they come running all the way back to the bush — it's only half a mile. They love trampling in the snow. Even the youngest children can hang the empty buckets from the trees. By the time they're ten or twelve, they can start emptying the buckets from the trees.

Most of the smaller maple syrup operators would say, "It's more for the fun of it than it is for the money." But it's still good to have some money to pay for equipment. Last year we tapped about 500 trees to get about 150 gallons of syrup. So that's an average of just over one quart per tree.

The Red House

I built this house in 1985. My dad had a 200-acre farm, which he split in two, so I had to put up all new buildings. We had a work bee and built the main part of the house in just three days. It's got six bedrooms, a kitchen, bathroom, summer kitchen and living room. I made it red because that's my favourite colour, but if I had to build it again, I'd make it out of brick instead of tin siding. Bricks last longer and don't rust through. There are some brick homes around here over 100 years old. The green tin roof was a good choice, though. It's more expensive to install, but it is easier to put up and lasts longer. People might think it's noisy during a rainstorm, but it isn't. It's been a great joy to design and build my barn and house together exactly the way I want them.

A Busy
Sparetime

Sunday is considered a day of rest. You go to church, and visit somewhere or have people coming in. If we don't have company, then we spend the afternoon catching up on reading, writing letters, or going for a walk. Many young people get together on a Sunday afternoon for singing in four-part harmony — it's a form of recreation. Wintertime is not nearly so busy, so if one has an hour or so of spare time in the evening, you might knit, write letters or read to the children. Some girls are good at sketching and painting, while others make rugs, embroider or crochet.

Bush Lots

Bush lots are an important part of your farm because that's your wood supply for winter heating. If you take proper care of it, a bush lot can be self-sustaining. The average farm will usually have about ten acres of bush. You can get one bush cord — eight by eight by four feet — of wood per acre, and you would need about five bush cords a season for the average house. They say that one tree, twenty-one inches in diameter at chest height, will yield one cord. So you really only need five trees like that for one winter's worth of heating. It's best to cut your trees one to two years ahead, so they can dry out properly. We try to do our cutting in December, when the trees are dormant and before there's too much snow. The trees are cut into four-foot lengths and hauled back to the yard with horse and sleigh. It's dried for the summer, and then in fall we'll buzz them into smaller pieces for the stove.

I really enjoy the annual tree-cutting. It's quiet in the bush and gives you a chance to enjoy nature. But it's also dangerous, and it's easy to get hurt. The worst thing are dead branches falling down.

You never know when it's going to happen and you have no control. The other thing to watch for when you're cutting a tree is when it "barber-chairs" or splits up the trunk. It can kick back before you know it. Mostly, that happens because of poor cutting technique. You've either used too small a chainsaw or cut on the wrong angle. Hickory is the worst. The grain is too straight and it can split real easy.

I also enjoy the challenge of trying to improve my bush. How you cut your trees makes a big difference in the future. The first thing is to always clean up the deadwood. You should get rid of the poorer quality trees such as beech and poplar. Some trees, like ironwood, are more like weeds that will never grow more than three to six inches in diameter, so they're not worth much. You have to clear them out so the oaks, maples and ash have a chance to grow up to the canopy. Taking care of a bush is like taking care of field crop, except it takes longer to see the results.

The New Buggies

It used to be that most buggies were open, but it seems more and more people are going for the enclosed rigs. It started off with the older people, but we're realizing it's a more comfortable way to travel. Because the community is spreading out, we tend to travel greater distances. On really cold days, it helps to have an extra horse blanket folded under your feet for insulation. And if you're going on a long trip, sticking a vinegar jug filled with hot water by your feet really does wonders. The worst kind of weather is ice pellets with strong winds. The horses don't like that at all. I think it stings their ears. Even in an open rig, we can dress for most kinds of weather, but it's the horses you have to be concerned about.

When the boys turn fifteen, that's when they feel they are sort of on their own, and they start associating with the "young folks." Dad will provide them with their first horse and buggy so that they are free to go visiting after church on Sundays. It's something they really look forward to. Then around age eighteen to twenty-one, Dad will buy them their very own new rig. The boys get to customize it some. They decide what kind and how many lights they want, turn signals and flashers. It will cost about $3,000, but if they take care of it, it should last a lifetime. The main repairs are replacing new rubber rims and keeping the spokes in shape. You have to paint your buggy every few years, as well. You try to have your buggy cleaned up for Sundays — especially if you have a girlfriend!

Church
and After

Mennonite churches are the central part of our community. It's the place where we are all connected to each other. We have ten churches in our district and hold services on a rotating basis, so that on a given Sunday, only five or six will have services. We do this so that people who live further away don't have so far to travel each Sunday. That's especially important in winter. In fact, on an extremely cold Sunday morning, a minister will sometimes mention that they don't want to make their sermon too long because of their concern for the horses. But there's no clock in the church, and since they are used to preaching for a certain length of time — our services are about two hours long — in the end, they often preach as long as normal. We have winter blankets for the horses, but their legs and necks are still exposed, so it's best to get them back into a warm barn as soon as you can.

On nice days, I particularly enjoy our drive to church together as a family. If it's been an especially busy week, it's a chance for my husband and I to catch up on things and have a relaxing conversation. As the children get bigger, of course, you have to spend more time taking care of them. Often the moms will sit in the back with some of the children and the rest stay in front with Dad.

Our churches commonly seat about 400 people, but with special services such as funerals, we might have 600 or more. We use bench seats, so you can always add a few more to a row. If it's really crowded and the weather is nice, you can always just open the window and people can listen from outside.

After church, there's a very busy ten to fifteen minutes when some quick visiting gets done. That's when important news of the week is shared. It certainly makes you feel part of a larger community. We often use that time to invite people for Sunday lunch and visiting. But people will also just drop in by surprise. That's part of our tradition. The children will be looking out of the kitchen window, wondering, "Who's coming now?" Sometimes, we'll have twenty-five or thirty people here for lunch. The women all work together, and soon we've got the meal ready. If it's home church that Sunday, I try to have meat and salad ready ahead of time, just in case we get a crowd. Sometimes the biggest surprise is when no one shows up. Then my husband knows what he's going to be eating for the rest of that week!

Visiting in general is an important part of our tradition. Mostly it's done Sundays after church. When a couple first gets married, they try to visit all their aunts and uncles after the wedding. That will take a year or so. We especially try to visit all our relatives and other people in our age bracket. A rule of thumb is that when you visit a certain family, somewhere in the next two to five years they will return the visit. I hope we can keep this up for the future.

Sunday Picnics

One of the special things we do as a family is that several times during the summer, we will pack a picnic lunch and on a Sunday afternoon walk back to the bush. We have to pull our small wagon for Rufus — he's only one year old. We take along egg sandwiches, apples, bologna sandwiches, carrots, and off we go down the laneway. It's probably dark of the time we get back. Once, the boys found a newborn fawn in the bush. By the time we got there later, it was already gone.

The Joy of Flowers

We love growing flowers because they please the eye. Usually we gather annual seeds in the fall for the next season. Every year they come out with brighter colours. The petunias are the best in the bright neon colours. Not only do we enjoy the flowers in the garden all summer, we like fresh bouquets on the table as well. They can last just about the whole growing season. Families often sell flower bunches at the roadside for tourists, especially petunias. We just leave the flowers at the end of the laneway with a sign and a jar to put the money in. Last year we sold about fifty bouquets.

When I was a young teenager, I once challenged my mother about the reason for so many flowers. Later I visited a place where there wasn't a single flower. Then I understood, because that place looked so desolate and cheerless.

What a Fire!

The Grand River runs right though our farm. On summer holidays, when we were finished our work in the garden, Mom would let us go back to the river for a swim. I spent hours and hours there with my brothers and cousins. Because of the high waters during the spring flood, we would always have to install a new diving board each year.

In the evening, the older teenage boys would often join us after they had done their chores. Once or twice a summer, we had a wiener roast. This one time, we found an old tractor tire that had been washed down by the river. Someone got the bright idea that we should throw it on the fire. Most of us had come on our bicycles, but one of the boys had come with a horse and buggy and had tied the horse to an old thorn tree about thirty feet away from the fire. Something in the burning tire caused a pinging noise. Horses don't like fires to start with, and with this extra noise, this one just spooked. It tore off its rope and took off down the lane with the buggy bouncing behind it. The older boys jumped on their bikes and chased after it. And here were us smaller boys left behind with a fire that was getting bigger and bigger all the time. It is quite a situation, with the grass starting to burn and around the edge of the fire. We had lots of water in a river but nothing to bail it with except for an umbrella that had fallen out of the buggy. But that didn't work well, so some of the boys ran to a neighbour's barn and brought back pails, and we finally doused the fire. As a small child that fire seemed so huge to me.

The Barn-raising

O ne of the tragic things you might experience on the farm is a barn fire. Even when it's not your own barn, there's just a horrible feeling in the pit of your stomach. You feel utterly helpless, because there's usually nothing you can do, except maybe help get the animals out. You watch the fire and you're already thinking of the tremendous loss and all the work that will have to be done.

The amazing thing about a fire is how ferocious it is. A huge barn can withstand years of wind and hail and storms. Yet just one little spark can reduce that barn to smoking ruins in only two or three hours. It's devastating. Imagine the feeling of helplessness if the farmer had to do all the rebuilding alone. That's why community is important.

You look forward to the day of a new barn-raising. It helps you to overcome the tragedy of the fire and gives you a real sense of accomplishment. Over the years, I've probably been to about forty raisings, both for new barns and replacing barns lost by fire. They usually happen within one to two weeks of the fire. A tremendous amount of work gets done, and it's also a great day for visiting. You begin in the morning with the main structure, and by the end of the day the roof is finished. It's amazing what 200 men can do. When you're heading down the driveway on your way home, you turn around in the buggy, look at a barn that wasn't there in the morning, and feel a great satisfaction. It's a reminder that life goes on.

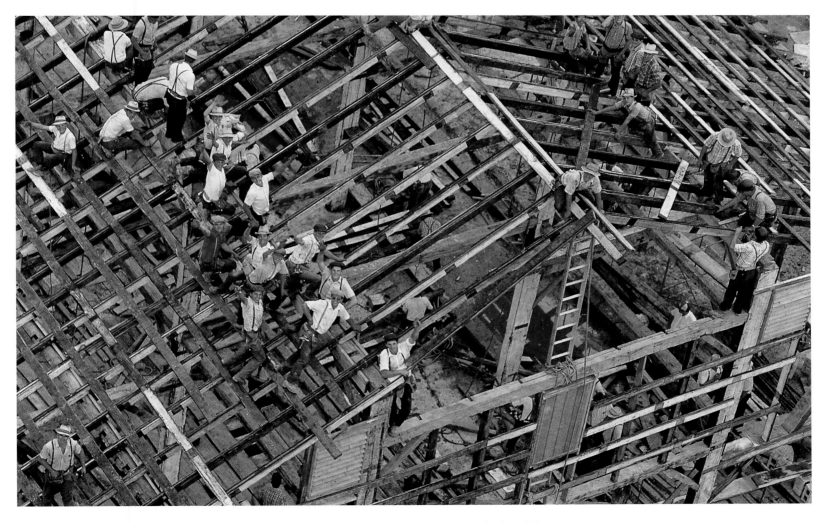

The day is a busy time for the women as well, with lots of work going on behind the scenes to prepare two full meals for those hungry men. It's a big team effort.

The barn-raisings are also special because they often pull together the much larger community. Dave Martins sometimes work alongside the Old Order Mennonites, and Catholic neighbours rub shoulders with Lutherans. There are no thoughts given to religious differences as we all work together.

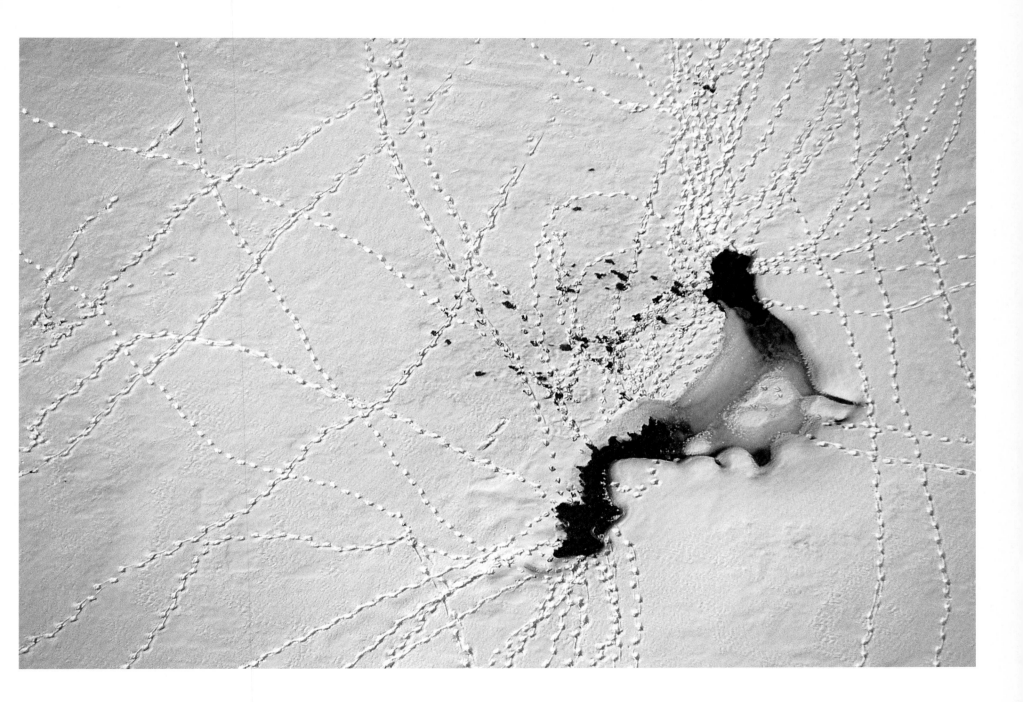

Ground Is Never Just Dirt

Spring is definitely my favourite time of year. After a cold, hard winter, the snow begins to melt and the green grass starts to show. If you take the time to watch, it's such a pleasure to see life slowly return to nature. We plant the seeds, and then we have to leave it to the Lord to see what the harvest will bring. For all the high-technology we have today, we still can't understand the miracle of growth. It's amazing, for example, that no matter which way the seed lies in the ground, the roots always go down and the shoots come up. It's important to realize that ground is never just dirt. It is life. It's the beginning of the entire food cycle. I was taught from young that everything we have is not ours, it's from God. Everything we do, we should do in a way that honours God. As farmers, we are just stewards of the land.

No One Does
That Anymore

I was probably one the first people in this area to make weed sprayers — something I started back in the 1940s. We used a forty-five-gallon drum for the tank and either powered it off the drive wheel or with a one-horsepower gas engine taken out of an old washing machine. It had a twenty-foot boom, and of course we pulled it with the team. I think we sold those first sprayers for about $150, and over the next twenty-five years I likely made four or five hundred of them. Most of the work was done in the winter, when we had more time on our hands, and quite often the farmer buying the sprayer would help me build it. Sprayers came along with the introduction of 2-4-D. That made a huge difference in controlling weeds. When I was a kid I used to spend hours hoeing fields. No one does that anymore.

Reluctant Exposure

People used to go to the big Kitchener market, but over the years that activity has shifted to the Waterloo market. Apparently it's considered one of the best outdoor markets in Canada. Some of our people sell goods there year-round — mostly things like maple syrup, summer sausage, potatoes and fruits in season. The market opens at 6:00 A.M., so people have to leave home between 4:00 and 5:00 A.M. if they're travelling by horse and buggy.

Generally, the market is an enjoyable experience. It's a good place to meet people, especially the regular customers that you get to know. One of our concerns is that the market is becoming more and more of an entertainment place, with rides and music. And in the summer, some people dress quite differently than us. We'd rather not have to expose our children to such things. And then there are tourists with their cameras. We prefer not to be photographed, and we are certainly not going to pose, but we realize that's going to happen sometimes because we've chosen to be in a public place.

Cows and Quotas

I t's becoming more and more difficult for a young person to take up farming. The only thing that makes it work for us is by having lower rates of interest from people in our community who have extra money to lend. It also helps to share equipment. There are four of us farmers who share one baler.

To set up a dairy farm today you could easily spend over a million dollars. Cows might only cost $2,000 each, but the quota for one cow right now is worth about $17,000. That's just for the marketing right to ship milk! Quotas only came into effect in the seventies, and they really don't have any true value, but they really make it difficult to become a dairy farmer. In fact, it's just about impossible unless the farm is passed down from the previous generation. Even then, the dads will sometimes help with the interest payments for the first few years after the son takes over. You have to see farming as a way of life, something you choose, because it doesn't make much sense economically.

It used to be that, years ago, hard work would get you through. That's still important today, but it's not enough. You also have to be a businessman, such as knowing what price to buy cattle at. You have no control over market prices when you sell them, so if you don't buy right, that makes all the difference as to whether you'll make a profit.

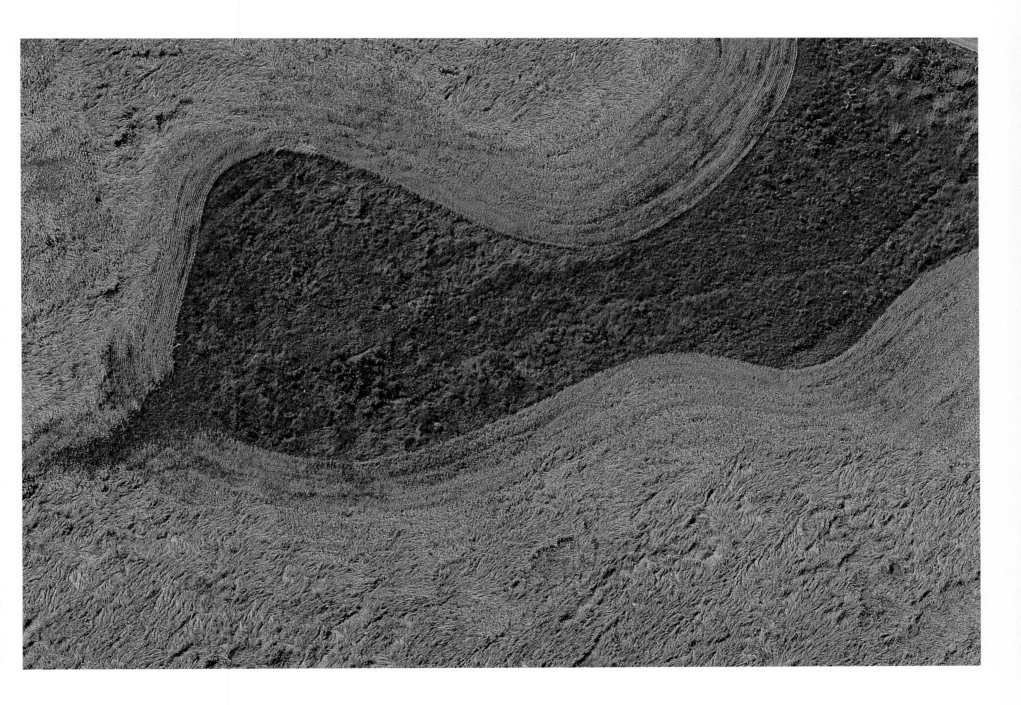

The Children's Garden

Many Mennonite families have small gardens for their children. My daughter just turned five this year, and she had her first garden. If there are several children, they'll possibly each have their own row to take care of. They will probably plant whatever they want, such as peas, corn, beans or watermelons, depending on what they like to eat. That way, they can take something from the garden whenever they want to and don't have ask the adults. Having their own garden is really important for them. Sometimes, after they've picked their own beans, they'll ask that their beans be put in a separate pot when we cook them for dinner. The hardest thing to teach them when they're cleaning the garden is between the weeds and plants. The children keep this up until they're ten or so, when they're old enough to work in the big garden.

The gardens are good for them. It teaches them to respect other people's things. They learn about having an investment in the whole cycle of planting and harvesting, and an appreciation of nature. When grandmother comes to visit, they are quite proud in asking, "Grandmother, come and see my garden." It's a good way for them to learn about work as well, because they can see the results of their efforts. I'm sure they get a deep satisfaction, because any time they are out playing they can run off to the garden and have a snack of fresh carrots or peas.

St. Jacobs

St. Jacobs has changed a lot from what it used to be. Thirty years ago, there was still a good grocery store, dry goods store, bank, hardware store, the mill, cider mill and blacksmith shop. We thought nothing of going there for most of our shopping. Most of the shops had tie posts for our horses, and there were hardly any tourists. But we seldom go there anymore. The shops we use are gone, and there are way too many tourists. I don't blame them for being there; I can understand the attraction of the place. But it's no fun going through town feeling like you're on display. I know we are different, but you get tired of being stared at. And particularly in summer, it's hard to drive with a horse and buggy when people are crossing the street everywhere. I don't think they realize how easily they could be hurt when they step out in front of us.

I believe there are still about seven Mennonite families living in St. Jacobs, and one of them owns a weaving shop. Several women make quilts, which are sold in the local stores, so we still have somewhat of a connection with the town.

The Eyes Have It

There's an old story about a hired man who was helping a farmer plant his potatoes. As you know, the eye of the potato is where the new shoot comes from. The farmer told the hired man to make sure all the eyes were pointing to the top when he put the potatoes in the hole. Well, the hired man was sure from his earlier experience working at home that this wasn't really necessary. So when the farmer wasn't looking, he planted an entire row with the potato eyes facing down. And when harvest came that year, his row was just as plentiful, so I guess he had the last laugh.

Once a Summer

One of the special things we like to do as a family is take a trip once a summer. We'll hire a van and driver and go for the whole day. So far we've been to Niagara Falls, Elora, African Lion Safari, and Cullen Gardens. Someday, I'd like to take a three-day trip to Agawa Canyon so my children can see real wilderness. One of the special memories of my own childhood is visiting Niagara Falls for the first time.

Seagull Schemes

I t's amazing to watch seagulls when you are ploughing in the fall. We think they must have some kind of system worked out. You can start ploughing without a bird in sight, and within half an hour, there are hundreds of them. They probably have scouts flying high overhead. When they see the fresh furrows, they know there's going to be lots of worms and bugs, and they send out their message, and one bird passes it on to the next until everyone shows up.

The Busiest Time

The busiest time of year happens from the middle of August until the end of September. The crops are ripening quickly, and almost every day there's a different fruit or vegetable to be canned or prepared for the freezer. The fieldwork is also in full swing, so we women often have to help with the morning and evening barn chores. And sometimes we also help out in the fields as well, by driving tractor for the baler or picking up stones. Grandmother is often busy babysitting the children, making lunches or doing the dishes for the rest of the family. There is a deep satisfaction in being on the "team" to bring in the harvest. It's a special time of year and makes us feel like we are surrounded by God's blessings.

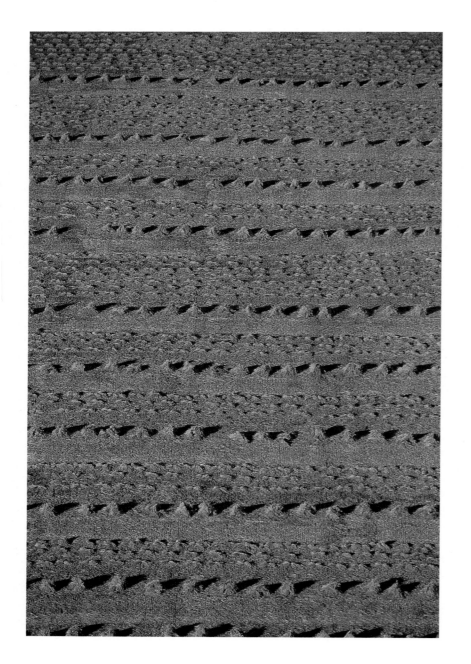

Summer's End

The air has a different kind of feeling in the fall. You can feel the summer winding down, things letting go. The trees in their autumn glory really catch at your throat. It's as though nature is saying, "Now it's time to relax and enjoy the results of a busy summer growing season." The orchard has a wonderful tangy smell from the apples as you walk through it, and the sky is often such a lovely blue, or else just as quickly a spit of rain comes.

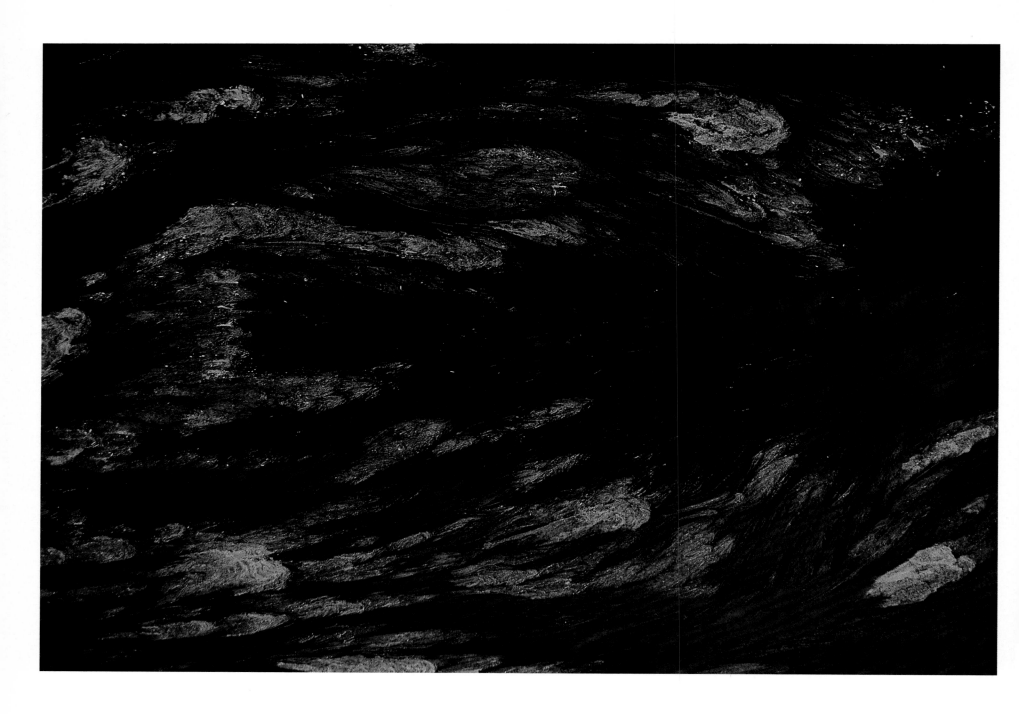

Harvesting a Reward

Harvesting feels like the reward for the effort. When the last field is finished, it is very satisfying. It's more than just an income, it marks another cycle and a time to count your blessings. It's very fulfilling. During the haying season, several farmers will often help each other because there's lots of hard work to do. Often the women will help by driving the baler, and sometimes they unload the bales onto the elevator.

Maple syrup harvest marks the end of late winter and early spring. People really look forward to this because it's such a good excuse to get out into the spring air, even though it's quite hard work gathering sap. The maple trees are so generous with their sap flow, and the product is so delectable.

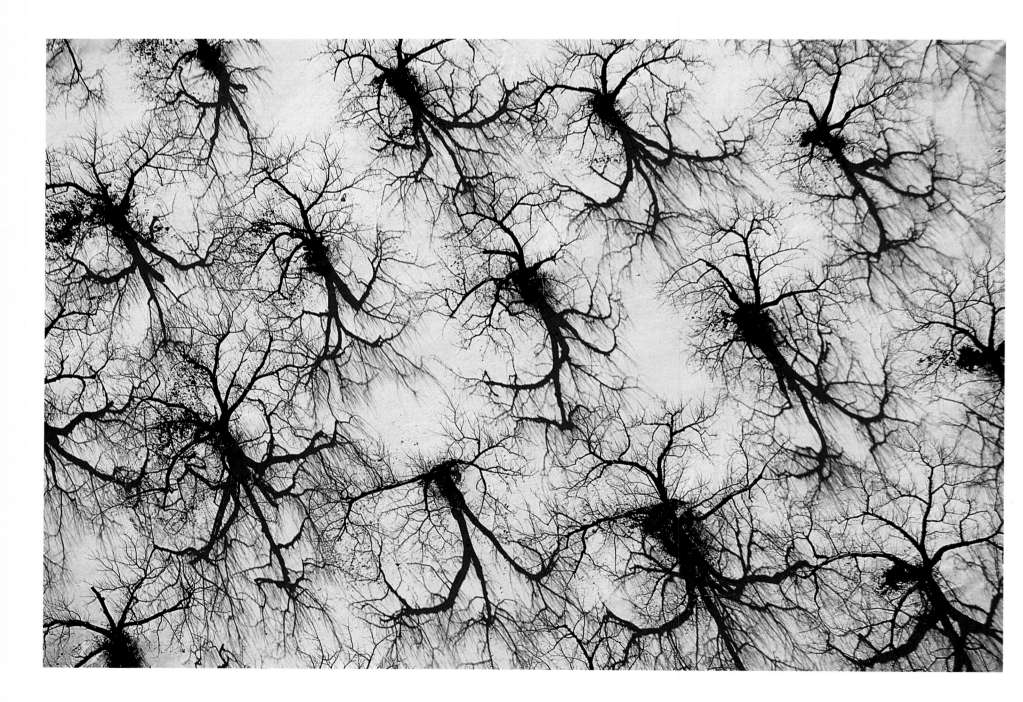

Canning

The gardens of course mean there's lots of canning to do. If you have a family of ten people to feed for winter, you might do up 700 or 800 jars. That would include carrots, cabbage, corn, peas, beans, strawberries, rhubarb, jams, tomato juice and tomato chunks. You try to make them last until the next season. My children really like ketchup, so we did up about 150 jars this year. We have our own meat and milk on the farm, so the only things we need to buy on a regular basis are things like flour, sugar and oatmeal.

It's such a pleasure to have fresh apple juice in the fall. Every year we make about forty gallons. One bag of apples will make about five gallons of juice. Your best juice comes from the sweet apples. What we like to do is mix Macintosh and Talman Sweets together.

Boys Driving Horses

Lots of boys start driving the teams for the grain harvest when they're about eight years old. First you to have to go with an older brother to learn how. It's not hard. You just tell the horses "Gitup" and "Whoa." Once a horse knows what that means, it will usually listen to anyone. To turn, you just pull one of the lines. You have to make sure you don't turn too sharp or you could break the tongue on the wagon, or maybe even tip the whole wagon over. If you drive on too steep a slope, the sheaves could fall off the load. And you must be careful not to drop one of the lines, otherwise one of the men on the ground has to hand it back up to you. I like driving the team. It feels good to know you're helping with an important job. I wonder if city boys could do this?

I started working with horses in the field a year ago, when I was twelve years old. At first, you only use two horses hooked up to cultivator. That's probably the easiest work to do. You have to be strong enough to haul in the reins. Dad still has to help us harness up, because we're not tall enough, even though we know how. You need more experience for a team of four horses, especially for ploughing. It's hard to keep them going straight. When I'm about sixteen, I'll be able to get my own horse and buggy and drive it on the road.

Bees and Bass

I would say cutting the corn in the fall is the hardest job on the farm. When it's tall and you spend the whole day picking the bundles off the ground and throwing them on the wagon, it's tough. Fortunately we have work bees, with maybe six or seven farmers working together. The more wagons there are, the more fun it is.

To get started today on a hundred-acre farm, you can easily spend a half million dollars, including the buildings and livestock. That means you have to have the least one or two other persons working out in order to make it pay. My work day begins at 5:00 A.M. and ends usually between eight and nine in the evening. I guess our main recreation is visiting on Sunday afternoons, though I might take off two or three days of the year to go fishing. Nothing tastes as good as fresh bass or redfin.

The Telephone

We've only had the phone in our community for about ten years. Years ago, we only used it for emergencies and it seemed very strange. I remember closing my eyes because I couldn't imagine talking to someone I couldn't see. Although the phone is good for making appointments, we certainly write fewer letters now. My daughter lives about seventeen miles away, and I used to write her about once a month. Now I just call. I'd be lucky to write one letter a year.

It's been a good life, farming. We had a dairy herd with up to thirty-two cows, and raised six children. Yes, it was hard work and it was good to see the end of the week. We were very glad the Lord said, "On the Sabbath you shall rest."

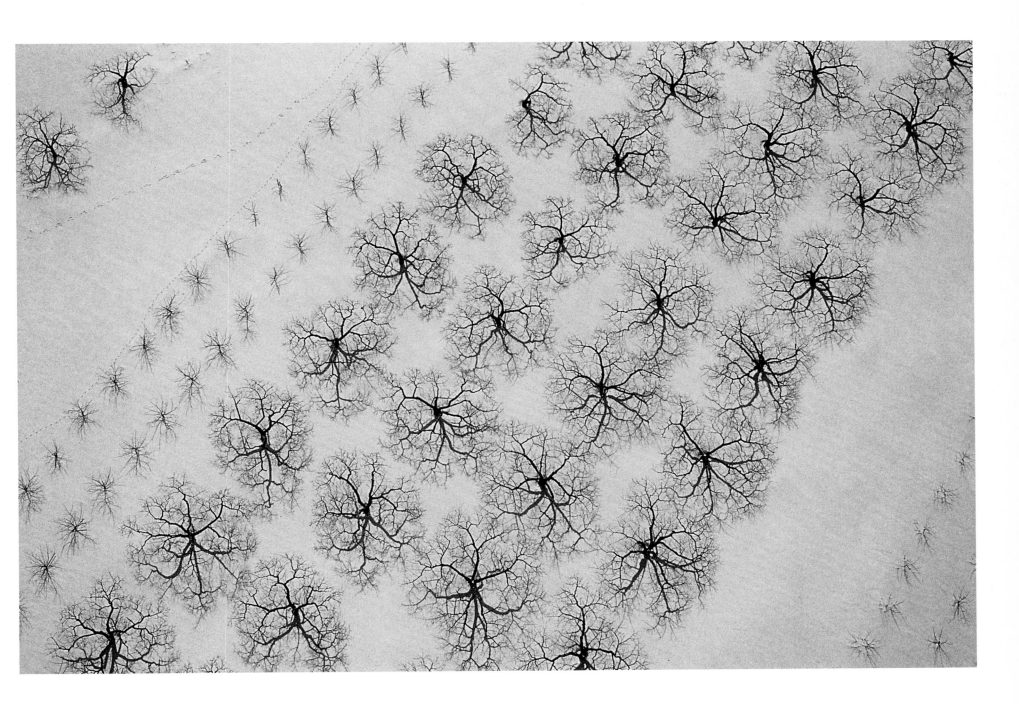

Weather Back When

There have been some hard winters. In 1934 it was between thirty and forty degrees below zero for a whole week. Another man and I were cutting wood in the bush, and it was so cold that the wedges would jump back out of the logs. We had to take along a pail of ashes and coal to warm up the wedges every so often. When we went back to the house for lunch we brought back more coal. What happens is the sap in the wood freezes and turns to ice, so when the wedge hits it just bounces back out. I've seen them fly out as far as two feet. That same summer it was so hot the sun burnt the blossoms on the oats, so it didn't germinate and we hardly got any grain at all.

The winters used to be much worse than they are now. The storms usually lasted three days and three nights. I can remember walking in the snowbanks and almost being able to touch the telephone lines. We had a bad snowstorm in 1947 when the snow was halfway up the belly on a horse. I had a good team of Percherons, Nelly and Dora, who had a lot of pep. I led the way, and three other neighbours' teams followed behind me. It took us a good hour to travel to Hawkesville, just down the road.

What Else Can We Do?

At present, about half of our community is eighteen years or younger. We have very few farms left to buy in our area, and the prices just keep going higher and higher. What are the young people going to do? I have three sons, but I can only pass my farm on to one of them. The banks won't lend money unless you have big collateral, so I can't buy two more farms. I'd rather see the people farming than have to work in town or in a big shop. That means they'll have to move away and start new communities. Mothers' hearts will bleed to see their daughters move away, but what else can we do?

The Mennonite Community

The Mennonite community is not a simple one to define. Waterloo County alone has over twenty different groups. They range from the conservative (e.g., Old Order Mennonites) to the moderates (e.g., Markham Mennonites) to the progressive groups (e.g. General Conference Mennonites). Since my own roots are based in a progressive community, the Mennonite Brethren, there is little today that allows me to identify with the conservative groups.

Our common ancestry springs from the early 1500s, when Menno Simons, a former Dutch priest, provided leadership to a Reformation group that had left the established Catholic church. Their basic tenets of faith included a belief in adult baptism upon confession of faith and a stance of pacifism. As the faith's followers grew larger, they became known as Mennonites.

The Old Order Mennonites in Ontario broke away from the mainstream group officially in 1889. They had begun migrating to Waterloo County in search of less expensive land in the early 1800s. Other groups, such as the Amish (a group completely separate from the Mennonites) immigrated directly to Ontario from Europe in order to escape compulsory military conscription. In 1917 a Mennonite splinter group led by David Martin broke away from the Waterloo Country group yet chose to remain settled in the same area. As noted in the introduction, I have focused my attention on these two conservative groups, the Old Order and Dave Martin Mennonites, in this book.

The stories and photographs originate in both groups, but with this bias: the stories tend to be mostly from the Old Order group, while the photographs favour the Dave Martin farms. I am grateful to both communities for having shared so freely with me.

Ultralights and Aerial Photography

Aerial photography is usually accomplished with small two- or four-place passenger planes, such as Cessnas, flying at altitudes of 1,000 feet or higher. My preferred aerial tripod is the ultralight, a lightweight, typically open-cockpit, slow-flying machine.

Ultralights date back to the late 1970s, when aspiring aviators attached little go-kart engines to foot-launched hang-gliders. Wheels were soon added, engines grew larger, and some of today's ultralights are not unlike small Piper Cubs. In my estimation, however, bigger and faster do not mean better, for the slower the flight, the more one has a chance to see.

Most of the photographs in this book were taken from the cockpit of a fourteen-year-old Canadian-made Beaver RX-550 two-place ultralight. Powered by a fifty-horsepower modified snowmobile engine, it cruises comfortably at fifty miles per hour. Thanks to the low stall speed, a 600-foot runway is sufficient, even with the extra weight of a passenger. Any newly cut pasture or grainfield is a potential runway, allowing me to literally "drop in" on my Mennonite friends. I land, and bicycles arrive from neighbouring farms, barefoot children charge across open fields to visit. I feel tremendously fortunate to live at time when flight is so accessible.

Aside from a narrow plastic windshield, my cockpit is completely open, allowing an unencumbered view. I can photograph from either side with equal ease, and by banking into a moderate turn, I can also photograph straight down. These vertical shots (such as those found on pages 51 and 65) are the most dramatic. They are also the most difficult to take. Depending on my altitude, I may have less than a second to compose and grab the shot. Add some turbulence, and the intended photograph may become too risky or even impossible. I often complete four or five passes and take a dozen pictures, hoping perhaps just one shot will meet my expectations.

The combination of simultaneous low-level flight and photography is a demanding discipline. It doesn't seem much easier even with years of experience. A complete focus is essential, for reasons of both survival and artistic intent. My best shooting is done while flying solo, without the distraction of an enthusiastic co-pilot.

There is an irony to the process of aerial photography, especially in the pursuit of artistic images. The gift of flight enhances the third dimension of space in our usual earthbound existence. But what we gain as an experience, we lose perceptually. In fact, the higher our altitude above the earth, the flatter the world below becomes. At 100 feet, a cornfield exhibits no obvious height. At 500 feet, farm buildings and trees have vertical scale mostly because of our conditioned response. Even the majestic Rockies, when viewed from the window of a commercial jetliner at 40,000 feet, appear surprisingly two-dimensional.

Fortunately, the aerial photographer can re-establish this missing vertical element by the effective use of side-lighting. It creates shadow detail, and therefore the perception of depth. For this reason, the hour after sunrise and before sunset, with its long shadows, are the moments of magic light. Rarely have any of my photographs shot midday qualified as keepers.

All the photographs in this book were taken with Canon 35mm cameras using Fuji Sensia 100 ISO amateur slide film. A polarizing filter was used for strong colour saturation. Most of these images were captured with one of two fixed focal lenses, a normal 50mm and a 135mm telephoto. More recently, I have switched to the Canon A2 auto-focus lens system, and now use two zoom lenses for my aerial work, a 28–70mm and 80–200mm. These lenses, with their amazing automatic focusing capability, make my work considerably easier, especially at low altitudes.

The picture of this tree would have been extremely difficult to take except for this autofocus technology. I cruised past this solitary oak on a midday flight, and an inner voice said, "Look. Look closer." I banked left, turned my zoom lens to its maximum 200mm setting and had time to grab only one shot as the tree flashed by just feet away. The emerging leaves hadn't yet had time to hide the tree in their green blanket, and the branches flowed black and graphic. I could look right through this painting and see dandelions scattered in the green pasture below. I pulled the ultralight hard through a 180-degree turn, back for another pass and another shot. Four more times I zoomed by and hoped just one photograph would do justice to this vision.

Photography can be a humbling experience. Why, after having seen thousands of similar trees, did I only recognize this perspective, this beauty, this time? For every picture I discover, how many do I fail to see? How aware am I, really, in my observation of this world? The wisdom of Marcel Proust comes to mind: "The real voyage of discovery consists not in seeking new landscapes, but in having new eyes."

I also wonder what sense compels me to "look closer." It is not a conscious decision, but flows naturally from somewhere within. All people can hone their skills to interpret beauty, but the wellspring of creativity, I believe, is fundamentally God-given. I feel blessed that I possess a visual curiosity of the world and have the opportunity to share its beauty with others.

Photographing this sunset was all about timing. I had just seconds to capture this image before it slipped away. It was nearing dark when I took off, after visiting a friend, for the short flight back to my hangar and the end of the day's flying. I climbed over the treeline and was immediately dazzled by the fullness of this sunset and the fact that it appeared to be setting exactly at the end of Highway 86. While climbing for altitude to set up the shot, I quickly glanced at the date on my watch. It was July 26. It occurred to me that every year, on this exact date, precisely at 9:24 P.M., the sun would rest here on this highway. It was as though man and nature had collaborated on this unusual timepiece. Wings level now, I steadied my telephoto lens with both hands and had time to squeeze off only three or four shots before the light disappeared. I turned and headed back to the farm, still surprised by the intensity of the moment just passed, and sensing the transience of my life in God's great framework of Time and the Universe.

The Book

When I first started photographing Waterloo County, it was not my intent to publish a book. The photographs were taken for my own pleasure, because of their inherent beauty. I fly primarily for two reasons: to share the experience of flight and to marry my passions for flight and aerial photography. In twelve years of shooting in my Waterloo County backyard, I have taken several thousand photographs. Despite regular and ruthless editing, my "final edit" file just kept growing larger. But while editing down my massive collection of images, I eventually realized how varied they were, and from this grew the idea of sharing the images in book form.

What would the text be? That question was largely answered by my having published a previous bestseller, *Us Little People*, a book about Mennonite children. In it, the children generously gave me stories they had written, stories that in a simple but powerful way gave clear insight into their world. Would their parents consider doing the same for this book? As I soon found out, they were not particularly interested in writing the stories themselves. Fortunately, they were willing to talk and to allow me to capture their words in my notebook.

Absence of self-centredness and vanity are important virtues to Mennonites. Having their names attached to a specific story might very well suggest something less than humility. When I gave them the assurance that individual names would not be used, the stories flowed much more spontaneously. You can likely infer from the writing the gender and approximate age of the teller. From there, one can only imagine the teller's name — Cleason, Jacob, Henry, Rebecca, Salome, Mary.

The one quiet regret I have carried with me for the last several years is that many times I've wished that I could share the experience of flight with the Mennonites themselves. They are the weavers of their earthly tapestry. They should be the first to see it displayed in all its splendour from an aerial vantage point. From subtle comments, I sense the interest is often there, but our flights together are not meant to be, because their church forbids such activities, which are seen as frivolous and unnecessary. My only consolation lies in knowing that some of my Mennonite friends will see this book. Vicariously then, we will fly together and share in our common delight of this land.